KU-036-375

For the Children's Book Council of Australia with thanks for the title and the poem – W.C.

For Hannelie and Charlotte – P.G.

The publishers would like to thank the following for permission to include
copyright material reproduced in this book.

John Agard: 'No Answer', copyright © 1985 John Agard by kind permission of John Agard, c/o Caroline Sheldon Literary Agency Ltd. Clare
Bevan: 'Tell Me, Tiger', copyright © Clare Bevan 2006, from Poems about Fire, compiled by Andrew Fusek Peters,
Evans Brothers Ltd, 2006. Reprinted by permission of the author. Valerie Bloom: 'Something Comes', copyright © 2000
Valerie Bloom, from Hot Like Fire (originally The World Is Sweet) published by Bloomsbury Children's Books.
Reprinted by permission of the author. Dionne Brand: 'Wind'. Material from Earth Magic, poem by Dionne Brand,
with illustrations by Eugenie Fernandes, used by permission of Kids Can Press Ltd., Toronto, Canada. Text © 1979, 2006
Dionne Brand. Paul Bright: 'The Old Windmill', copyright © Paul Bright 1999, reproduced with permission of Curtis Brown
Group Ltd. Tony Bradman: 'Leave the Whales Alone, Please', copyright © 1991 Tony Bradman. Reproduced by permission of
The Agency (London) Ltd. All rights reserved and enquiries to The Agency (London) Ltd, 24 Pottery Lane, London W11 4LZ.
Alan Brownjohn: 'We Are Going to See the Rabbit…', copyright © Alan Brownjohn. Alan Brownjohn's Collected Poems is published
by Enitharmon Press. Tony Chen: 'Question', copyright Tony Chen 1972, from Run, Zebra, Run, Lothrop, Lee, 1972. Reprinted by permission of
the Estate of Tony Chen. Alison Chisholm: 'Wind Farm Haikus', copyright © 2006 from Poems about Air, compiled
by Andrew Fusek Peters, Evans Brothers Ltd, 2006. Reprinted by permission of the author. Gina Douthwaite: 'Captivating or
Captive Creature' from What Shape's an Ape? by Gina Douthwaite, published by Red Fox. Reprinted by permission of The Random House
Group Ltd. Felice Holman: 'Who Am I?', copyright © Felice Holman 1970, from At the Top of My Voice, and Other Poems by Felice Holman,
Scribner, 1970. Reprinted by permission of the author. Elizabeth Honey: 'All the Wild Wonders', © Elizabeth Honey, The Moon on the Man,
first published Allen & Unwin, 2002. Penny Kent: 'The Sun', © Penny Kent, first published in Poems about Fire, compiled by Andrew Fusek
Peters, published by Evans Brothers Ltd 2006. Reprinted by permission of the author. Ian Larmont: 'Grey and White and Black', copyright ©
1999. Wes Magee: 'Snagger's Pond', copyright © 2006. Brian Moses: 'Dreamer' ©
Brian Moses from Hippopotamus Dancing and Other Poems by Brian Moses, Cambridge University Press, 1994. Owgden Nash:
'Song of the Open Road', copyright © 1932 by Ogden Nash. Reprinted by permission of Curtis Brown, Ltd. Grace Nichols:
'For Forest', copyright © Grace Nichols 1988, reproduced with permission of Curtis Brown Group Ltd. Judith Nicholls: 'What is One', ©
Judith Nicholls 1994, from Storm's Eye by Judith Nicholls, published by Oxford University Press. Riad Nourallah: 'An Alphabet for the Planet',
copyright © Riad Nourallah, from Footprints On The Page, compiled by Fiona Waters, Evans Brothers Ltd, 1998.
Reprinted by kind permission of the author. Andrew Fusek Peters: 'Man, the Mad Magician', copyright © Andrew Fusek Peters,
first printed in Poems about Water, compiled by Andrew Fusek Peters, Evans Brothers Ltd, 2006. Reprinted by permission
of the author. Virginia Driving Hawk Sneve: 'I Watched an Eagle Soar', copyright © 1989 by Virginia Driving Hawk Sneve.
All rights reserved. Reprinted from Dancing Teepees: Poems of American Indian Youth by permission of Holiday House, Inc.
Benjamin Zephaniah: 'Natural Anthem' from Funky Chickens by Benjamin Zephaniah, Viking, 1996.
Copyright © Benjamin Zephaniah, 1996. Reproduced by permission of Penguin Books Ltd.

The publishers apologise to any copyright holders they were unable to trace and would like to hear from them.

Quarto is the authority on a wide range of topics.
Quarto educates, entertains and enriches the lives of
our readers—enthusiasts and lovers of hands-on living.
www.quartoknows.com

All the Wild Wonders copyright © Frances Lincoln Limited 2010
This selection copyright © Wendy Cooling 2010
Illustrations copyright © Piet Grobler 2010

First published in Great Britain and the USA in 2010 by Frances Lincoln Children's Books
This paperback edition published in 2017 by Frances Lincoln Children's Books
74-77 White Lion Street, London N1 9PF
QuartoKnows.com · Follow our blogs at QuartoKnows.com

All rights reserved

ISBN: 978-1-84780-994-0

Illustrated with pencil and watercolours

Printed in China
2 4 6 8 9 7 5 3 1

MIX
Paper from
responsible sources
FSC® C008047

WENDY COOLING is a highly respected figure in the children's book world. A former teacher, she is the founder of the Bookstart programme and has edited story collections for Puffin, Orion and Collins, poetry anthologies for Franklin Watts and has retold traditional tales for Barefoot Books. Wendy lives in Hertfordshire.

PIET GROBLER grew up on a farm in Limpopo, South Africa. After working as a church minister, he made a career in illustration and now lectures at the University of Worcester. He is the recipient of many international illustration awards, including the IBBY Honours List.

C016358017

All the Wild Wonders

Poems of our Earth

Edited by Wendy Cooling

Illustrated by Piet Grobler

Frances Lincoln
Children's Books

Contents

All the Wild Wonders   8

When the Sun Rises   10

The Sun   11

What is One?   12

For Forest   13

Throwing a Tree   14

Song of the Open Road   15

The Prayer of the Tree   16

Evening   17

Question   18

Grey and White and Black   19

Snagger's Pond   20

Night   22

Dreamer   23

Man, the Mad Magician   24

A Robin Red breast in a Cage   24

If I Was a Bird   25

The Eagle   26

I Watched an Eagle Soar   27

Wind   28

Something Comes   29

Wind Farm Haikus   30

The Old Windmill   31

An Alphabet for the Planet   32

Tell me, Tiger   34

Captivating Creature   35

Captive Creature   35

Spring Fjord   36

No Answer   37

Leave the Whales Alone, Please!   38

From *Paradise Lost*   39

If You Ever   39

"We are Going to See the Rabbit..."   40

Who am I?   42

Natural Anthem   43

About the Poets   44

Introduction

The poems in this anthology show two sides to our world and its future. They celebrate the beauty of 'all the wild wonders', but they also point out danger – and where we see danger, we need to think and to act.

We all have a place in the wholeness of the world, and we all have a responsibility. The poets in this book are not just thinking seriously, but also joyously reflecting the wonder of the world in the words they have given us. Their writing questions, entertains, describes and touches our imaginations – and above all it offers hope.

My hope is that just one of the poems lingers in your mind long after the book has been put down.

Enjoy!

Wendy Cooling

All the Wild Wonders

For you my sweet babe
I wish fish in the sea
Birds in the trees
Tigers in jungles
And all the wild wonders
All the wild wonders
For you my sweet babe

For you my sweet babe
I wish carpets of wildflowers
Beetles and butterflies
Bright birds of paradise
And all the wild beauty
All the wild beauty
For you my sweet babe

For you my sweet babe
I wish wind for the albatross
Clear flowing rivers
Forests of giants
And all the wild wonders
All the wild wonders
For you my sweet babe

For this wish to come true
We have much work to do
All the wild wonders
All the wild wonders
For you my sweet babe

Elizabeth Honey

Australia

When the Sun Rises

When the sun rises, I go to work,
When the sun goes down, I take my rest,
I dig the well from which I drink,
I farm the soil that yields my food,
I share creation, kings can do no more.

Anonymous

China (2500 BC)

The Sun

Our
Earth would fit a
million times inside the
Giant sun; a ball of burning
Gases giving light to everyone.
The sun's a star that pulls the
Planets round and round and
Round by gravity, the force that
Holds us firmly to the ground.
Without the sun, there'd be no
Life, no creatures, grass or
Trees. We need the
Sun – without its heat
Everything would
Freeze.

Penny Kent

England

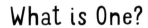

What is One?

One is the sun,
a rhino's horn;
a drop of dew,
a lizard's tongue.

One is the world,
a lonely whale;
an elephant's trunk,
a monkey's tail.

One is an acorn,
one is a moon;
one is a forest
felled too soon.

Judith Nicholls

England

For Forest

Forest could keep secrets
Forest could keep secrets

Forest tune in everyday
To watersound and birdsound
Forest letting her hair down
to the teeming creeping of her forest-ground

But Forest don't broadcast her business
no Forest cover her business down
from sky and fast-eye sun
and when night come
and darkness wrap her like a gown
Forest is a bad dream woman

Forest dreaming about mountain
and when earth was young
Forest dreaming of the caress of gold
Forest roosting with mysterious eldorado

and when howler monkey
wake her up with howl
Forest just stretch and stir
to a new day of sound

but coming back to secrets
Forest could keep secrets
Forest could keep secrets
And we must keep Forest

Grace Nichols

Guyana/England

13

Throwing a Tree

The two executioners stalk along over the knolls,
Bearing two axes with heavy heads shining and wide,
And a long limp two-handled saw toothed for cutting great boles,
And so they approach the proud tree that bears the death-mark on its side.

Jackets doffed they swing axes and chop away just above ground,
And the chips fly about and lie white on the moss and fallen leaves;
Till a broad deep gash in the bark is hewn all the way round,
And one of them tries to hook upward a rope, which at last he achieves.

The saw then begins, till the top of the tall giant shivers:
The shivers are seen to grow greater each cut than before:
They edge out the saw, tug the rope; but the tree only quivers,
And kneeling and sawing again, they step back to try pulling once more.

Then, lastly, the living mast sways, further sways: with a shout
Job and Ike rush aside. Reached the end of its long staying powers
The tree crashes downward: it shakes all its neighbours throughout,
And two hundred years' steady growth has been ended in less than two hours.

Thomas Hardy

England

Song of the Open Road

I think that I shall never see
A billboard lovely as a tree.
Perhaps, unless the billboards fall,
I'll never see a tree at all.

Ogden Nash

USA

The Prayer of the Tree

You who pass by and would raise your hand
        against me, hearken ere you harm me,
I am the heat of your hearth on the cold
        winter night, the friendly shade screening
        you from summer sun,
And my fruits are refreshing draughts
        quenching your thirst as you journey on.
I am the beam that holds your house, the
        board of your table, the bed on which you
        lie, the timber that builds your boat.
        I am the handle of your hoe, the door of your
        homestead, the wood of your cradle,
        the shell of your last resting place.
I am the gift of God and the friend of man.
You who pass by, listen to my prayer and
        Harm me not.

Anonymous

Evening

In the woods full of evening the nightingales are silent,
The rivers absorb the sky and its fountains,
Birds return to the indigo shores from the shadows,
A scarlet pearl of sunshine in their beaks.

Ahmet Hasim

Translated by N. Menemencioglu

Turkey

Question

As asphalt and concrete
Replace bushes and trees,
As highways and buildings
Replace marshes and woods,
What will replace
The song of the birds?

Tony Chen

USA

Grey and White and Black

They've changed our living spaces
To grey and white and black.
What used to be our wetlands
Are concrete and tarmac.
Where once a stretch of water –
A motorway, or worse,
A man-made, hard-core desert,
An antiseptic curse.

Where once a thriving reed-bed,
A place to rest and feed
When winter time was over,
A place to stretch and breed,
Is now a dry, hard greyness,
No vestige of a lake.
It won't come back…
No more tarmac,
For everybody's sake.

Ian Larmont

England

Snagger's Pond

Snagger's Pond was dying.
There was bad pollution.
So, what could we do?
What *was* the solution?

We dragged out bicycle tyres,
Rusty wheels, soggy plastic bags,
An old brolly, worn trainers,
Tangled twine and rotting rags.
We pulled out a Wellington boot,
A headless doll, slimy stones,
Handfuls of decaying leaves,
Bats and balls, beanbags and bones.

Then we hosed in water for hours,
Introduced scores of water snails,
Aquatic plants, green duckweed,
Frogspawn, and pebbles in pails.
We put in a pair of newts
And fish – a dozen or more –
Then watched the minnows, ghost carp
And small shubunkins explore.

Snagger's Pond was dying.
There was bad pollution.
So, we cleaned and restocked.
We *found* the solution.

Wes Magee

England

Night

Silently sleeps the river.
The dark pines hold their peace.
The nightingale does not sing,
Or the corncrake screech.

Night. Silence enfolds.
Only the brook murmurs,
And the brilliant moon turns
Everything to silver.

Silver the river,
And the rivulets.
Silver the grass
Of the fertile steppes.

Night. Silence enfolds.
All sleeps in Nature
And the brilliant moon
Turns everything to silver.

Sergei Esenin

Translated by G. Thurley

Russia

Dreamer

I dreamt I was an ocean
and no one polluted me.

I dreamt I was a whale
and no hunters chased after me.

I dreamt I was the air
and nothing blackened me.

I dreamt I was a stream
and nobody poisoned me.

I dreamt I was an elephant
and nobody stole my ivory.

I dreamt I was a rainforest
and no one cut down my trees.

I dreamt I painted a smile
on the face of the earth
for all to see.

Brian Moses

England

Man, the Mad Magician

Said the money-man "We must have oil!
And that's my final word!"
How magical and tragical his final act
As the seagull became a blackbird.

Andrew Fusek Peters

England

A Robin Red breast in a Cage

A Robin Red breast in a Cage
Puts all Heaven in a Rage.

William Blake

England

If I Was a Bird...

If I was a bird
I would like to fly in the sky
so that everyone could see me.
I could fly in and out of the clouds and caves.
There'd be just one pest in my life –
that's a man with a gun to shoot me,
Him I wouldn't like.

If I was a man and not a bird,
I'd never shoot at birds
Because a bird is lovely to see
when it's flying.
If I was a man I'd just watch,
not shoot.

Anonymous

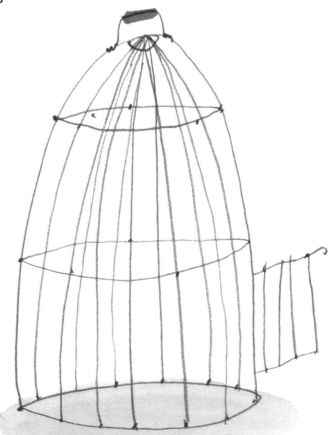

The Eagle

He clasps the crag with crooked hands;
Close to the sun in lonely lands,
Ring'd with the azure world, he stands.

The wrinkled sea beneath his claws;
He watches from his mountain walls,
And like a thunderbolt he falls.

Alfred Lord Tennyson

England

I Watched an Eagle Soar

Grandmother,
I watched an eagle soar
High in the sky
until a cloud covered him up.
Grandmother,
I still saw the eagle
behind my eyes.

Virginia Driving Hawk Sneve

USA

Wind

I pulled a hummingbird out of the sky one day
     but let it go,
I heard a song and carried it with me
     on my cotton streamers,
I dropped it on an ocean and lifted up a wave
     with my bare hands,
I made a whole canefield tremble and bend
     as I ran by,
I pushed a soft cloud from here to there,
I hurried a stream along a pebbled path,
I scooped up a yard of dirt and hurled it in the air,
I lifted a straw hat and sent it flying,
I broke a limb from a guava tree,
I became a breeze, bored and tired,
and hovered and hung and rustled and lay
     where I could.

Dionne Brand

Canada

Something Comes

Over the mountains,
Like thunder of drums,
Shaking the leaves from trees,
Something comes.

Down through the valleys
With the bellow of bombs,
Alarming the cows and sheep,
Something comes.

Up through the forests
The frightened air hums,
For tearing it in pieces,
Something comes.

Moving up the driveway
With a noise that numbs,
Crumbling the paving stones
Something COMES!

Valerie Bloom

Jamaica/England

Wind Farm Haikus

A silver forest
Of trunks spears sky. Angled boughs
Sweep stiff, catch the wind.

No sap oozes, no
Leaves curl; but the forest yields
Electric harvest.

Alison Chisholm

England

The Old Windmill

Catch the wind, just for an instant
Catch the wind, then let it go
Take a breath from nature's forces
Snatch it from the winds that blow

Catch the wind, with wood and canvas
Massive sails stretch and fill
Slow and creaking, faster, stronger
Breathing life into the mill

Ancient beams transmit the motion,
Wood-hewn bearings slap and moan,
Pulleys lift, and gear-wheels trundle
Powering the wheel of stone

Grain is caught, and crushed, and powdered
Sacks are filled, and stored for need
Winds that once caressed the wheat field
Grind the goodness from the seed

Catch the wind, just for a moment
Catch the wind, then let it go
Yesterday, today, tomorrow
Power from the winds that blow

Paul Bright

England/Spain

An Alphabet for the Planet

A for air.

The gentle breeze by which we live.

B for bread.

A food to bake and take – and *give*.

C for climate.

It can be warm, it can be cold.

D for dolphin.

A smiling friend no net should hold.

E for Earth.

Our ship through space, and home to share.

F for family.

Which also means people *everywhere*.

G for green.

Colour of life we'll help to spread.

H for healthy.

Happy and strong, no fumes with lead.

I for ivory.

The elephant's tusks, his *own* to keep.

J for jungle.

A rainforest. No axe should creep.

K for kindly.

To everyone, gentle and good.

L for Life.

It fills the sea and town and wood.

M for Mother.

She may feel hurt, but loves us all.

N for nest.

A tiny home for chicks so small.

O for ozone.

It shields our earth from harmful rays.

P for Peace.

My happy dream, the Planet says.

Q for quiet.

Where no loud noise can get at you.

R for recycled.

Old cans and cards as good as new.

S for Sun.

The nearest star. It gives us light.

T for tree.

A grander plant, a green delight.

U for united.

Working as one to put things right.

V for victory.

Winning over disease and war.

W for water.

The whole earth drinks when rainclouds pour.

X for xylophone.

Music from wood – the high notes soar!

Y for yummy.

Those tasty fruits organically grown.

Z for zoo.

A cage, a condor – sad, alone.

Riad Nourallah

Lebanon/England

Tell me, Tiger

After William Blake

Tell me, tiger,
What became
Of your stripes as bright
As a jungle flame?

What became of
Your glittering eyes
Sharp as stars
In the jungle skies?

What became of
Your flickering tail
Curved and coiled
As a jungle trail?

What became of
Your fiery heart
When the jungle patterns
Ripped apart?

When the jungle smoke
Swirled ghostly blue,
Tiger, what became
Of you?

Clare Bevan

England

Captivating Creature

Elephant roaming in forest, on grassland,
using her trunk like a hand and an arm,
sucking up water to spray as a shower,
wafting palm ears when the sun gets too warm,
dusting herself with a trunkful of dry sand,
ripples of wrinkles encompassing eyes.
On thick pillar legs she's at peace with her power,
At ease with a brain hardly mammoth in size.

Captive Creature

Elephant restless in circus, in zoo,
pacing and pawing at concrete and bar,
longing for freedom and wide-open-spaces,
leading processions, bedecked with howdah,
drooping with feathers and wearing a tutu,
learning, on two legs, to balance and dance.
Juggling with balls. Being put through such paces
doesn't give dignity much of a chance.

Gina Douthwaite

England

Spring Fjord

I was out in my kayak,
I was out at sea in it,
I was paddling
very gently in the fjord Ammassivik.
There was ice in the water
and on the water a petrel
turned his head this way, that way,
didn't see me paddling.
Suddenly nothing but his tail,
then nothing.
He plunged, but not for me:
huge head upon the water,
great hairy seal,
giant head with giant eyes, moustache
all shining and dripping,
and the seal came gently toward me.
Why didn't I harpoon him?
Was I sorry for him?
Was it the day, the spring day, the seal
playing in the sun
like me?

Traditional Inuit song

Greenland

No Answer

Once the seals had skins
shiny wet as a new anorak.

Now their skins have a rusty look
of an old car part.
The star has fallen out of their eye.

The seals have no answer
to the question
of poisonous waste.

O laughter
walk on water
that the seals may smile again.

John Agard

Guyana/England

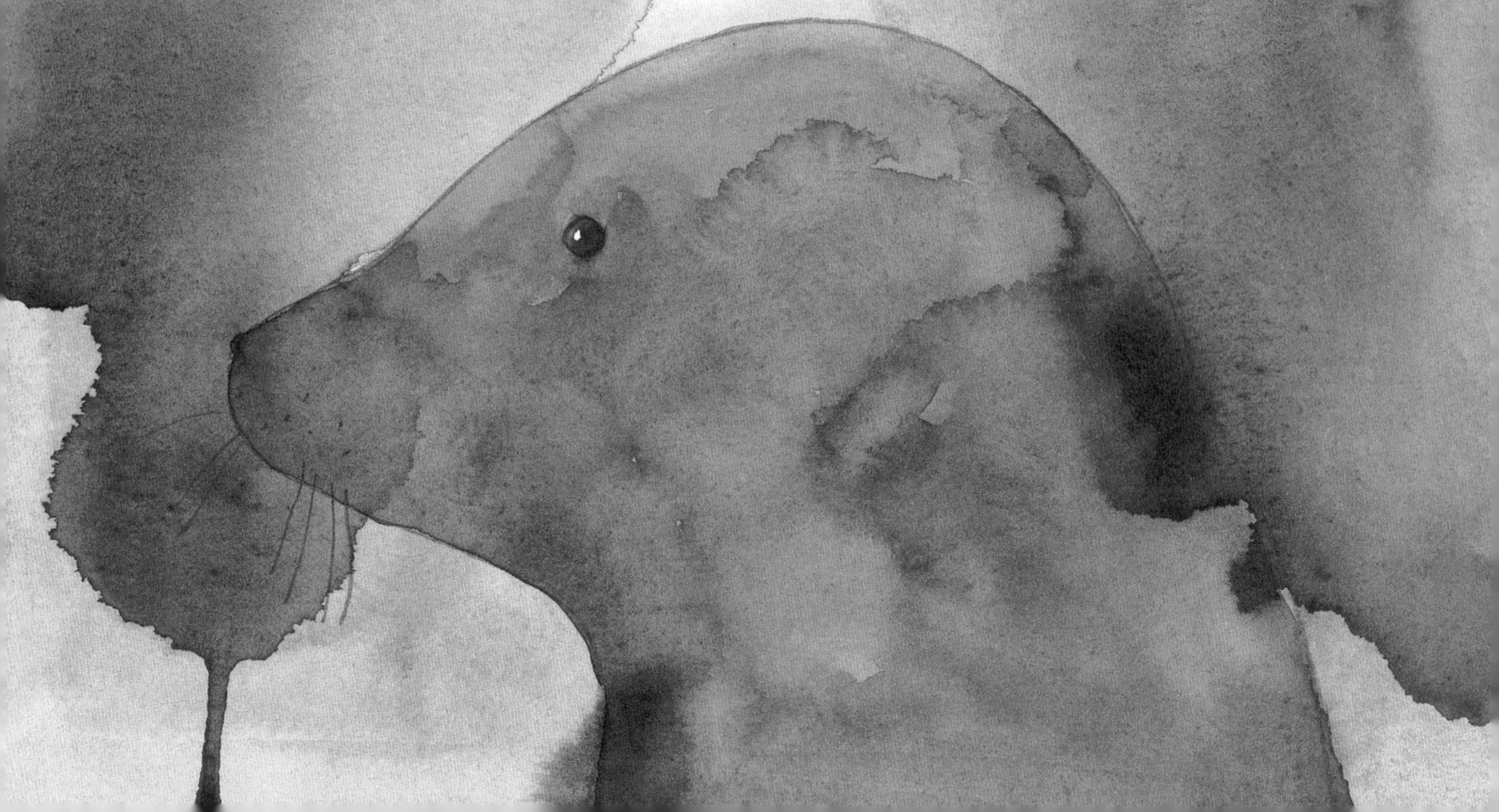

Leave the Whales Alone, Please!

Leave the whales alone, please,
They don't do any wrong;
They swim in every ocean,
And fill them with their song.

Leave the whales alone, please,
Like us, they've got a brain;
But if we don't start using ours,
We won't see them again.

Leave the whales alone, please,
We need them in the seas;
We need their life and beauty,
And all they need is peace.

Leave the whales alone, please,
Let them live their lives,
Let them leap, and swim, and sing –
Let the whales survive!

Tony Bradman

England

From *Paradise Lost*

There Leviathan,
Hugest of all living creatures,
In the deep
Stretched like a promontory,
sleeps or swims,
And seems a moving land;
and at his gills
Draws in, and at his breath
spouts out a Sea.

John Milton

England

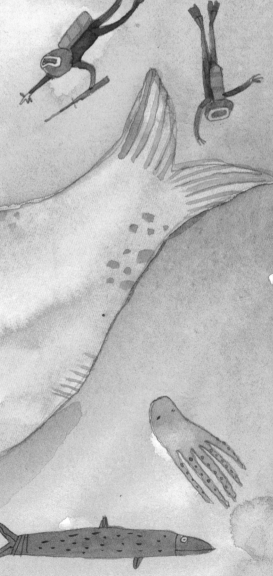

If You Ever

If you ever ever ever ever ever
If you ever ever ever meet a whale
You must never never never never never
    You must never never never touch its tail:
For if you ever ever ever ever ever
    If you ever ever ever touch its tail,
You will never never never never never
    You will never never meet another whale.

Anonymous

'We are Going to See the Rabbit...'

We are going to see the rabbit,
We are going to see the rabbit.
Which rabbit, people say?
Which rabbit, ask the children?
Which rabbit?
The only rabbit,
The only rabbit in England,
Sitting behind a barbed-wire fence
Under the floodlights, neon lights,
Sodium lights,
Nibbling grass
On the only patch of grass
In England, in England
(Except the grass by the hoardings
which doesn't count.)
We are going to see the rabbit
And we must be there on time.

First we shall go by escalator,
Then we shall go by underground,
And then we shall go by motorway
And then by helicopterway,
And the last ten yards we shall have to go
On foot.

And now we are going
All the way to see the rabbit,
We are nearly there,
We are longing to see it,

And so is the crowd
Which is here in thousands
With mounted policemen
And big loudspeakers
And bands and banners,
And everyone has come a long way.
But soon we shall see it
Sitting and nibbling
The blades of grass
On the only patch of grass
In – but something has gone wrong!
Why is everyone so angry,
Why is everyone jostling
And slanging and complaining?

The rabbit has gone,
Yes, the rabbit has gone.
He has actually burrowed down into the earth
And made himself a warren, under the earth,
Despite all these people.
And what shall we do?
What *can* we do?

It is all a pity, you must be disappointed,
Go home and do something else for today,
Go home again, go home for today.
For you cannot hear the rabbit, under the earth,
Remarking rather sadly to himself, by himself,
As he rests in his warren, under the earth:
'It won't be long, they are bound to come,
The are bound to come and find me, even here.'

Alan Brownjohn

England

Who am I?

The trees ask me,
And the sky,
And the sea asks me
Who am I?

The grass asks me,
And the sand,
And the rock asks me
Who I am.

The wind tells me
At nightfall,
And the ram tells me
Someone small.

Someone small
Someone small
But a piece
of
it
all.

Felice Holman

USA

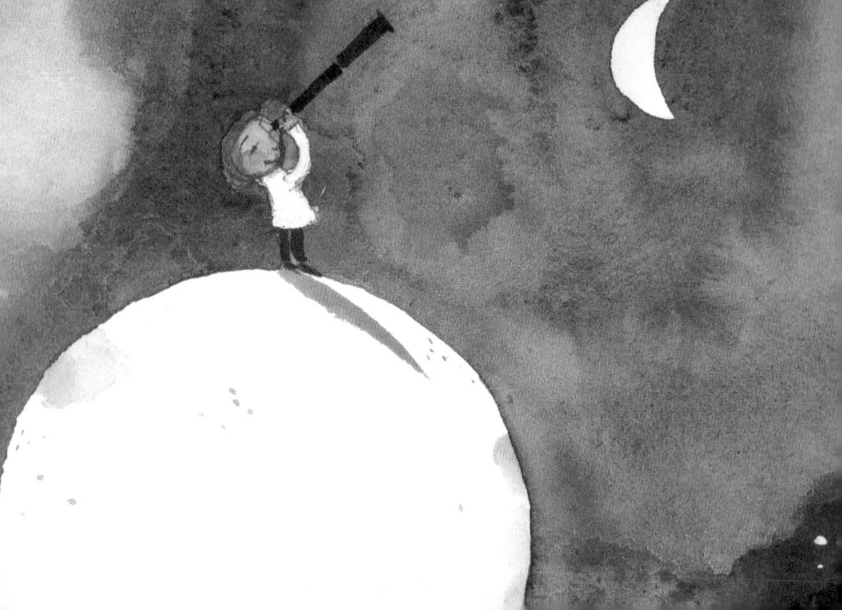

Natural Anthem

God save our gracious green
Long live our glorious scene
God save our green.

Dis ting is serious
Do it for all of us
Save our asparagus,
God save
Our
Green

Benjamin Zephaniah

England

About the Poets

John Agard, who grew up in Guyana, is popular throughout Britain as a playwright, poet and performer, winning many awards for his perceptive, humorous writing.

Clare Bevan, who used to work as a primary school teacher, writes stories, plays and poems packed with magic and mystery, which she performs in schools.

William Blake (1757–1827), an early Romantic poet, painter and prophet of a better world, is one of England's greatest poetic voices. He wrote the poem *Jerusalem*.

Valerie Bloom grew up in a Jamaican village and now lives in the UK, travelling widely and performing her lively English/Jamaican poetry.

Tony Bradman, who is is best known for his *Dilly the Dinosaur* series, has written over 90 books for children.

Dionne Brand was born in Trinidad, and her poetry resonates with Caribbean rhythms. She now lives in Canada.

Paul Bright is a plastics expert who started writing stories for his children when they were young. He now lives and writes in Spain.

Alan Brownjohn was a schoolteacher and lecturer before becoming a novelist. He now devotes himself to the cause of poetry.

Tony Chen (1929-94) was born of Chinese parents in Jamaica and lived in the United States. He wrote poetry, painted and sculpted as well as writing and illustrating children's books.

Alison Chisholm has had over 500 poems broadcast or published. She enjoys helping others to improve their creative skills in workshops and readings.

Gina Douthwaite lives in a barn on the Yorkshire Wolds. As well as writing poetry, she also runs Shape Poetry school workshops and creative writing workshops.

Virginia Driving Hawk Sneve is a teacher, editor and poet living in South Dakota whose work is strongly influenced by her Sioux heritage.

Sergei Esenin (1895-1925) was one of Russia's most loved Revolutionary poets. He was inspired by animals, the forests around him and village folklore.

Andrew Fusek Peters is a poet and performer who has written and edited over 70 books for children. His poems feature in the Poetry Archive.

Thomas Hardy (1840–1928) was a much-loved poet and novelist whose writing is strongly influenced by nature and life in his native Dorset.

Ahmet Hasim (1884–1933) was an influential poet in Turkey in the early 20th century, a time of great change in the country's social, political and economic life.

Felice Holman was born in the United States and is a widely published and respected novelist and poet.

Elizabeth Honey is one of Australia's most popular authors with her award-winning fiction, picture books and poetry.

Penny Kent has had her children's poems published in over 45 anthologies. She is currently living in India.

Ian Larmont has been writing humorous children's poems for over twenty years. A keen conservationist, he still likes planting trees now and again.

Wes Magee has become a firm favourite with children for his poems, which he composes in a hut in his garden on the North York Moors.

John Milton (1608-74) wrote at a time of huge political change in England. One of the country's most renowned poets, he is best known for his epic *Paradise Lost*.

Brian Moses started writing poems when he realised he wasn't going to make it as a rock star, and since then has had over 150 books published.

Ogden Nash (1902–71) was an American poet best known for his light verse making use of clever rhymes and wordplay.

Judith Nicholls is one of Britain's best-known poets for children, with over 50 books published.

Grace Nichols' Guyanan upbringing has influenced her work with its strong oral traditions. She now lives in England writing for adults and children.

Riad Nourallah has taught at the Universities of Beirut, Cambridge, Salford, Durham and the United Arab Emirates, and now teaches at the Diplomatic Academy of London.

Alfred Tennyson, 1st Baron Tennyson (1809–92) was Poet Laureate for 42 years and remains one of England's most popular poets.

Benjamin Zephaniah is a celebrated Rasta performance poet whose work, with its humorous overtones and serious message, is greatly influenced by Jamaican culture.

ALSO BY WENDY COOLING AND PIET GROBLER FOR FRANCES LINCOLN CHILDREN'S BOOKS

A IS AMAZING!
Poems about Feelings

Amazing, bored, excited, magical, naughty, sad, zestful....
you can feel any way you like in this exciting collection of
poems about feelings from A to Z.

ISBN: 978-1-84780-513-3

Frances Lincoln titles are available from all good bookshops.
You can also buy books and find out more about your favourite titles,
authors and illustrators on our website: www.franceslincoln.com